CASEBOOK

Author team
Caroline Clissold and Kate Pink

OXFORD
UNIVERSITY PRESS

Great Clarendon Street, Oxford OX2 6DP

Oxford University Press is a department of the University of Oxford.
It furthers the University's objective of excellence in research,
scholarship, and education by publishing worldwide in

Oxford   New York

Auckland   Cape Town   Dar es Salaam   Hong Kong   Karachi
Kuala Lumpur   Madrid   Melbourne   Mexico City   Nairobi
New Delhi   Shanghai   Taipei   Toronto

With offices in

Argentina   Austria   Brazil   Chile   Czech Republic   France   Greece
Guatemala   Hungary   Italy   Japan   Poland   Portugal   Singapore
South Korea   Switzerland   Thailand   Turkey   Ukraine   Vietnam

Oxford is a registered trade mark of Oxford University Press
in the UK and in certain other countries

British Library Cataloguing in Publication Data

Data available

ISBN-13: 978-0-19-835039-2
1 3 5 7 9 10 8 6 4 2

Printed in China by Hing Yip

Acknowledgements

All cartoon character artwork including cover and title page by mr-dunn studio

All illustrations by Olwen Fowler with the exception of **p30**c, **p30**bl, **p40**t, **p40**c, **p43**cr, **p45**cr,
p48t, **p54**, **p55**l, **p55**c, **p55**cb by Ian Naylor c/o Illustration Ltd; **p46**c Neil Gower; **p47**c James Cauwood

The publisher would like to thank the following for permission to reproduce photographs:
p14cb Brian Carter/Photolibrary.com; **p68**cb, 68tl GeoScience Features Picture Library.
Studio photography by MM Studios. All other photos by Classet/Hemera/OUP.

DISCLAIMER: Every effort has been made to contact copyright holders of any material in this book.
Any omissions will be rectified in subsequent printings if notice is given to the publishers.

The authors and publisher would like to thank all the schools, consultants and advisers who have helped
to trial, pilot and review the **Maths Investigator** resources. Please see the *Getting Started Guide* for full details.

Contents

Each case
is a new
problem to solve.
Use your maths
skills to help you.

9

The case of the hidden treasure

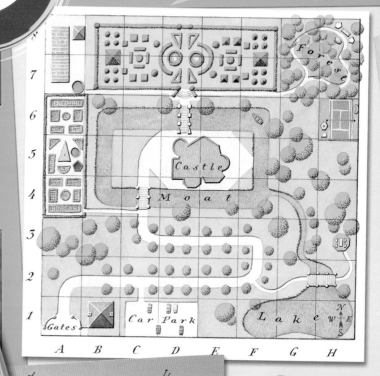

TOP SECRET

TOP SECRET

TIPS FOR PROBLEM SOLVING

1 Read and identify the question
2 Decide where to start
3 Follow your plan (order and
   record your work)
4 Review and choose your
   next move
5 Solve and check your answer

one or
...rtices.

North on the bridge
and down the stairs.
...t shapes do ...u see up in the air?
Time to ...
can yo...
You must ...
it ...

It is not
a prism.

Go to the hexagon where
you find no right angles.
Walk through to the
quadrilateral then
...e the one with less
...than 3 sides.
...rt your search.

Look at
the clues. Think
carefully to
work out what
they mean.

Spy phon...
PDA x1...

4

Welcome to MI.
Are you ready to join our
top secret spy agency?

M is the head of MI. She will send you messages as you work on each case.

AGENT I.C. SAND

The MI agents are waiting for your help!

T SPY
53 13
EXPIRY 10
J.BLOND

balcony
bedroom
landing
toilet
closet
balcony
lounge
hall
bedroom
library
bedroom
storage

landing
music room
toilet
dining room
living room
reception hall
sitting room

Grade 4

Agent security clearance

1 a Combine these shapes to make as many new shapes as you can.

Ready to move to the next level? Find out by taking a security clearance check.

faces
edges
vertices
uare
ngular
ngular

MATHS INVESTIGATOR MI MATHS INVESTIGATOR

3

The case of the missing spy

Hi M,

Gone on holiday.

Got a plane yesterday

morning and left the country!

Somewhere in Europe.

Jane x

M
MI3 HQ

The case of the missing spy

The Cheap Flight Company

FLIGHTS

Flights	Italy	Croatia	Norway	France	Greece	Cyprus	Spain	Switzerland
One way	£220	£150	£140	£175	£120	£130	£100	£160
Return	£300	£200	£230	£250	£235	£260	£175	£270

ACCOMMODATION (7 DAYS)

Room	Italy	Croatia	Norway	France	Greece	Cyprus	Spain	Switzerland
Single	£140	£180	£130	£175	£120	£90	£120	£100
Double	£200	£220	£160	£250	£160	£110	£215	£120

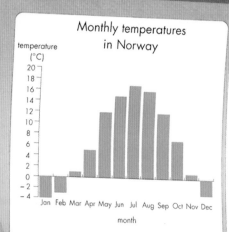

Monthly temperatures in Norway

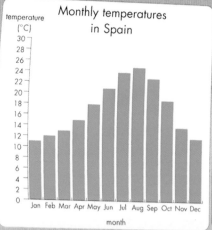

Monthly temperatures in Spain

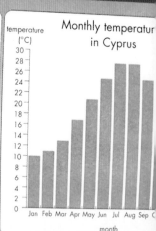

Monthly temperatures in Cyprus

From: Jane Blond
To: M
Subject: Holiday

Hi M!

I'm having a fabulous time in this out of the way little place, swimming and sunbathing. The weather is so hot! Apparently it's hot here most of the time, it's even quite warm during the winter. I'm getting a lovely suntan.

LOL Jane

JANE BLOND

...ot a very comfortable ...e room.

Monthly temperatures in Greece

Jan Feb Mar Apr May Jun Jul Aug Sep Oct Nov Dec
month

Destination	Depart UK	Arrive
Paphos, Cyprus	11:25 a.m.	5:50 p.m.
Larnaca, Cyprus	9:10 a.m.	3:45 p.m.
Malaga, Spain	9:30 a.m.	1:15 p.m.
Kos, Greece	11:00 a.m.	5:00 p.m.

- good place to go for weekends
- short flight from Gatwick Airport, London
- journey from the airport to hotel takes about 35 minutes by bus

let gus ta

be pe ca ers

?

asp po ms ans

toes

PP bb

age tuce

A=2 B=4 C=6

4 ara

ya

SECRET CODE

ACCESS C-41

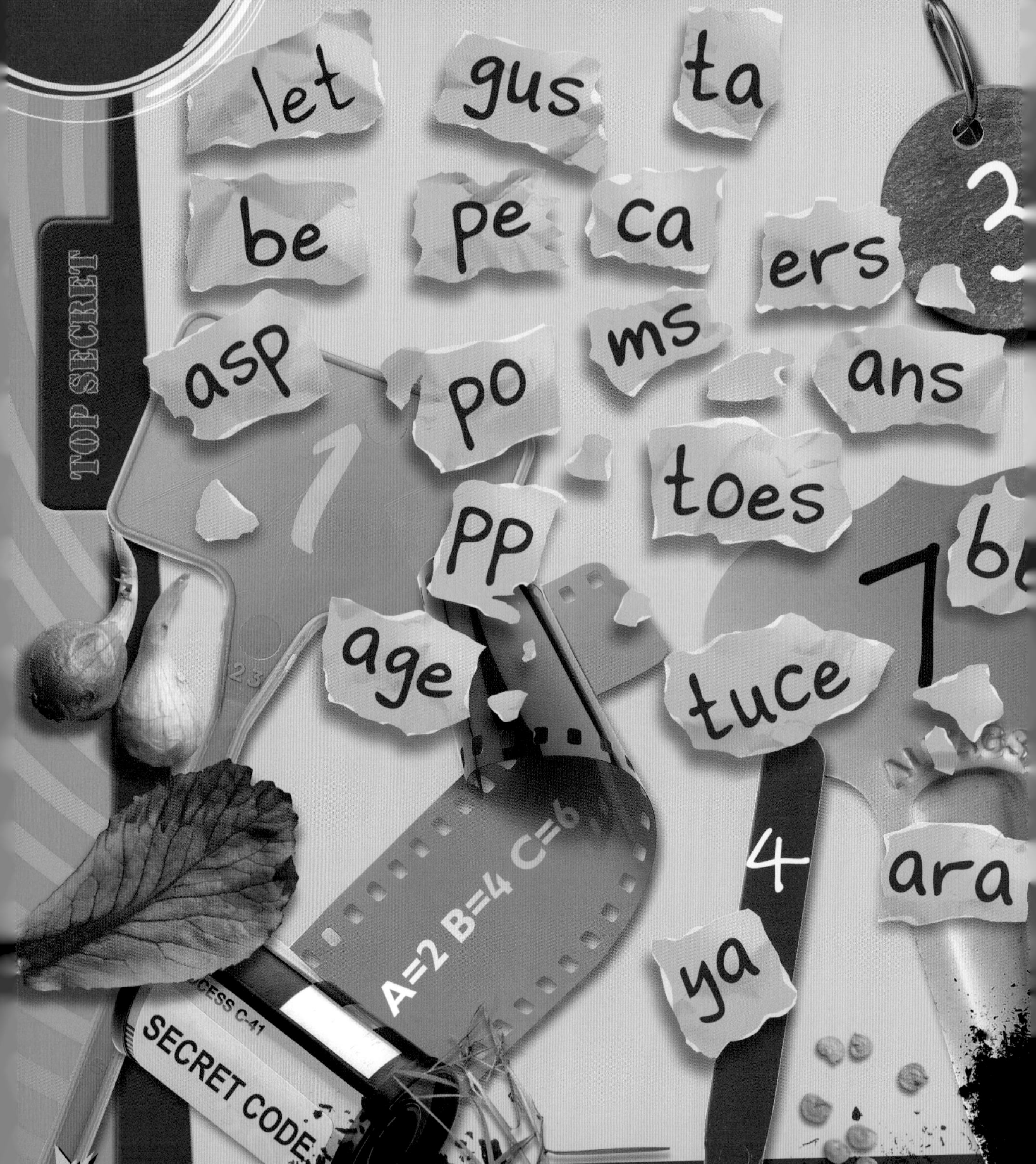

Vegetables will be double in size when they are fully grown in 4 weeks.

TOP SECRET

The width of each plant will be half its length.

The lettuce must be beside the cabbage but nothing else.

The asparagus and the pepper can't be beside the cabbage, bean or potato.

The potato must be next to the cabbage and yam.

Each area must fit closely to the size of the vegetable planted in it.

NOSE PEG

3

TOP SECRET

Special Agent Equipment and

£15
one-piece swimsuit

£10
T-shirt

£20
bikini

sun block

£14.50
socks

£30
wetsuit

£40
lifejacket

fins

£10.99
mask and snorkel set

£45
cylinder

£4.99
flip flops

khaki shorts

Clothing and equipment budget

Super Agent Rain: £150 each phase of mission

Super Agent Drop: £150 each phase of mission

APPROVED

From: M
Sent: Yesterday
To: Rain S.A, Drop S.A.
Subject: Operation Save Puddle

Agents,

PHASE: 1
DESTINATION: Andes Mountains, Peru
WEATHER: between −7 °C and 4 °C
GOAL: Retrieve 5 flowers from lantana bush

Hurry!
M

Pa

Can you help
Agents Rain and Drop
save Puddle the cat?

AGENT RAIN

AGENT DROP

...hing Company

£15.99

shirt

£25

desert boots

£12.50

balaclava

£28

sunglasses

£25

mountain-climbing
trousers

£32

khaki trousers

£40

jacket

£8.99

flask

£10

sun hat

£25

fleece

£45

climbing boots

£4.50

thick woolly hat

£35

waterproof
jacket

£12.50

gloves

£4.50

scarf

£13

rope

... Secrecy Guaranteed

RAPIDO WORLDWIDE DELIVERY

We want:

Rain	Drop
Sun hat, flip flops	fleece, desert boots, sunglasses

SCHEDULES

Depart	Arrive	Notes
London 10:25 a.m.	Peru 11:45 p.m. (UK time)	Peru is 5 hours behind UK time
London 8:30 a.m.	Sahara 1:50 p.m. (UK time)	Parts of the Sahara are 2 hours ahead of UK time
London 8:30 a.m.	Maldives 10 p.m. (UK time)	The Maldives are 5 hours ahead of UK time

OPERATION SAVE PUDDLE: Phase 2
AGENTS: Rain and Drop
DESTINATION: Sahara Desert, North Africa
WEATHER: 50°C during day, cold at night
GOAL: Retrieve 5 needles from cactus (see photo)

OPERATION SAVE
PUDDLE: Phase 3
AGENTS: Rain and Drop
DESTINATION: Small island
in the Maldives
WEATHER: Between 27°C
and 31°C during day,
warm at night
GOAL: Retrieve dropped
petals of 4 exotic flowers
and 32 seeds from exotic
seed pods.

AGENT RAIN

AGENT DROP

- Each flower has 6 petals.
- Each pod has 8 seeds in it.

NAME: DROP, S.A.	
Final Destination: London	9:20 a.m. Friday
	11:20 a.m. Friday
Leave: Maldives	1 hour 30 minutes
Arrive: Sri Lanka	
Transit:	12:50 p.m. Friday
Leave: Sri Lanka	3:15 p.m. Friday
Arrive: Dubai	11 hours
Transit:	2:15 a.m. Saturday
Leave: Dubai	
Arrive: London	
Total journey time: 26 hours	

MI3,
Back by 8 a.m.
or on to Plan B?

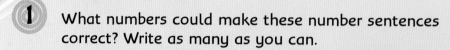
TOP SECRET

1. What numbers could make these number sentences correct? Write as many as you can.

   a ☐ + ☐ = 20

   b ☐ + ☐ = 100

2. Jane Blond wants to buy 7 postcards, 5 souvenirs and 9 stamps. How many items does she buy altogether?

3. a Write 3 numbers that add up to 21.

   ➡ Write 4 more sets of 3 numbers that total 21.

4. What other ways could you add these numbers to get the same answer?

   $24 + 36 + 29 = 89$

5. Write all the number sentences you can using these 3 numbers.

   35 **64** **29**

6. Find the missing numbers. Write as repeated addition or subtraction sentences.

   a ☐ x 6 = 24

   c ☐ ÷ 3 = 5

   b ☐ x 10 = 90

   d 42 ÷ ☐ = 7

7. Agent Rain went shopping and spent £1·45 on lettuces, 36p on an apple and £1·24 on a pumpkin. How much did she spend altogether?

Are you ready to move to the next level? Answer these questions to find out. Show your methods in your exercise book.

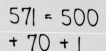

571 = 500 + 70 + 1

8   **a**   Make five 3-digit numbers using these digits.

    b   Order them from smallest to largest.

    c   Partition each number.

1 5 7
2 4

9   **a**   Estimate how long your classroom is.

    b   Estimate how long your pencil is.

10   How much water is in this jug?

11   How heavy is the sand on these scales?

12   What time is it? Write down 3 ways to show it.

13 ➡ Use these digits to make 3-digit numbers that will total as close to 1000 as possible.

3 4 6
9 8

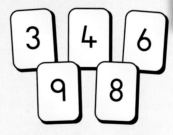

You can only use a digit once in a number!

14   Agent Quad found a shape shop. He went in to look around. The cubes cost £1·50, the cylinders £3 and the sphere £6. He spent exactly £12. What could he have bought? Find all the possibilities.

TOP SECRET

Agent Quad

Our unexpected holi~~day~~ has really shaped u~~s~~ into a great time. Do these remind you of anything? Don't wish you were here and won't see you soon,

Count Tri and *Countess Angl~~e~~*

P.S. Good luck replacing them (not!)

20

Can you cheer up Agent Quad by replacing his shapes?

STOLEN

AGENT QUAD

Have you seen these shapes?

They are 3D, have many faces and come in several colours. They may be in the company of this devious duo.

If you have any information, please contact M or Agent Quad at MI.

The case of the stolen shapes

The Birdwatcher

Sandbox Surprise

Clue 1: I have 1 face, no edges and no vertices.

Clue 2: I have 6 faces, 8 vertices and 12 edges. All my faces are the same shape.

Clue 3: I have 1 square face, 5 vertices and 8 edges. Some of my faces are triangles.

General

Want to make new friends and get fit?

Join the hoop club at the V.C.C. every Wednesday.

50p
entrance

Clue 4:
I have 6 faces, 8 vertices and 12 edges. My faces are 2 different sizes.

Clue 5:
I have 3 faces and 2 edges. My faces are 2 different shapes.

Clue 6:
I have 1 vertex and 2 different faces.

Hungry for more Brussels sprouts?

Come and pick your own
at Kooky Mo's Farm
(18 kg minimum)

The shape that is made from
squares is blue; its closest
shape is red. The one with
only one vertex is green and
the one with a square base
is yellow. The one that can
roll in any direction is brown.
The one that can only roll
in one direction is orange.

Found

One child's mitten,
pink and green
with hole in thumb.
Contact Beyant at
Hilltop Primary School.

Wanted

4 sorting posters – 2D,
hexagon, octagon, star,
quadrilaterals, irregular?

Sleepless Nights for Lo

by: Janna Lupo

Locals have been hearing
some strange things over
the past week, says police
constable Gaynor. He has
received over 10 phone
calls from local citizens
complaining of loud cackling
laughter and hiccupping late
into the night. 'I think it is
coming from the abandoned
manor,' suggests Terry Fence
of Appleton Lane. 'It's as if
the sound is being carried
on the wind. I can't sleep
a wink – and my parrot Kiki
could do without it as well.'
Police have investigated but
found only empty cans of
beans and shredded magazines.

Is anybody home?

AGENT QUAD

TOP SECRET

Party Specials

50 for

sausage rolls

pizza

5 for £10

orange juice

£2 per litre

pies

2 for 50p

baguette sandwichs

30 eac

cold cuts

£1 per platter

chicken sandwich

2 for 40p

potato salad

50p per bowl

tomato & feta salad

75p per bowl

eggs

10p each

fresh green salad

50p per bowl

smoked salmon sandwiches

30p each

couscous

£1 p bow

roasted vegetables

50p per bowl

chicken salad

80p per bowl

dips

15p each

Don't forget
- 50 people work at the base
- $\frac{1}{5}$ are vegetarians
- $\frac{9}{10}$ of the staff like dancing

Can you organize a surprise party for everyone at headquarters?

AGENT FRY-UP

crisps **10p** per bag

peanuts **15p** per bag

pa...

French bread sticks **25p** each

£1 bowl

coronation chicken

50p per bowl

wild rice salad

cucumber sticks **25p** per bag

£1 for 2 litres

fizzy drinks

15p each

mini quiches

satay **5p** each

vol-au-vents **10 for £2**

carrot sticks **25p** per bag

fruit salad **25p** per bowl

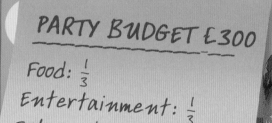

PARTY BUDGET £300

Food: $\frac{1}{3}$

Entertainment: $\frac{1}{3}$

Extras: $\frac{1}{3}$

APPROVED

mini burgers **24p** for 3

10 for 60p

spicy potato samosas

paper plates
10 for £1.00
20 for £1.50
100 for £5.00

knives
10 for 40p
20 for 80p
100 for £1.60

forks
10 for 50p
20 for £1.00
100 for £2.40

SALE
1/2 OFF ALL
PARTY
SUPPLIES

Flat Foot Band
For music and prices you won't beat!
Deposit: £5
£20 an hour

DJ Jive
fantastic offer!
Disco, disco, disco for as long as you want!
£1.60 per person

Dances R Us
Playing just for you
Special price: £60
plus 50p per person

DJ Dan Cing
Party, party, party!
£25 per hour, buy me for three and get a fourth hour free!
More hours £30 each

The Big Dance Band
We'll play at your party for up to four hours!
£18 an hour
Extra hours £25

serviettes
10 for 20p
20 for 32p
100 for 80p

spoons
10 for 40p
20 for 60p
100 for £1.80

AGENT FRY-UP

Start party at 6 p.m.
Finish at midnight?
Music for $\frac{1}{2}$ of the party?

balloons
10 for 20p
20 for 36p
100 for £1

streamers
10 for 6p
20 for 10p
100 for 60p

party poppers
10 for 20p
20 for 40p
100 for £1.20

fireworks
10 for £15
20 for £20
100 for £80

1 Use 4 of these words to help you complete the table.

sphere   cube   cuboid   cylinder   pyramid

shape	faces	vertices	edges	prisms (Y/N)
	5 – 1 square, 4 triangles	5	8	
	6 – all the same shape and size	8	12	
	3 – 2 different shapes, curved	0	2	
	6 – all the same shape but not always the same size	8	12	

2 Draw these shapes and describe their properties.

1 example

circle
semi-circle
square
rectangle
star

2 examples

pentagon
octagon
triangle
quadrilateral

- number of sides?
- right angles?
- lines of symmetry?

3 What is the number?

a $\frac{1}{2}$ of 40

b $\frac{1}{3}$ of 27

c $\frac{1}{4}$ of 32

d $\frac{1}{5}$ of 30

e $\frac{1}{6}$ of 18

f $\frac{1}{10}$ of 70

Are you ready to move to the next level? Answer these questions to find out. Show your methods in your exercise book.

4 Jane Blond wants to order 24 chicken satay sticks. How much will it cost?

5p each

75p per bowl

tomato & feta salad

satay

5 Agent Fry-up ordered 4 salads. How much did he spend?

6 Write all the x and ÷ number sentences you can using these 3 numbers.

40 **50** **8**

7 Agent Quad put his new collection of 36 shapes into jars. He put 4 shapes in each jar. How many jars did he use?

8 Agent Fry-up baked 48 cheese straws and stored them in boxes. Each box holds 10 straws. How many boxes did he use?

9 **a** Draw an array to show 4 x 8.

➡ Draw an array of 24 as many ways as you can.

10 **a** Make five 3-digit numbers using these digits.

4 **5** **2** **9** **4**

b Order them on a number line.

```
0                    452                         1000
|--------------------|----------------------------|
```

➡ Make 5 more 3-digit numbers and place them on your number line.

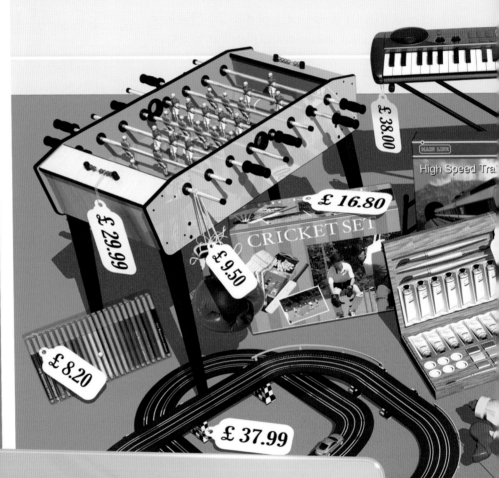

TOP SECRET

£ 38.00

High Speed Tra

£ 16.80

£ 29.99

CRICKET SET

£ 9.50

£ 8.20

£ 37.99

£ 19.

1000 Piece Ji

NAME: WILL E. FORGETMENOT
AGE : 8

LIKES _____ DISLIKES _____

- GETTING MESSY
- RIDING BIKES
- PLAYING OUTSIDE

- READING, PLAYING GAMES OR DOING PUZZLES FOR LONG PERIODS
- PLAYING WITH CARS OR TRAINS
- FOOTBALL AND MUSIC

COMMENTS: _____
OFTEN ON HQ GROUNDS IN AFTERNOONS. ALWAYS MUDDY WITH
SCRATCHED KNEES. CHEERFUL, BUT SCATTY.

Can you help Special Agent Forgetmenot buy a birthday gift for his son, Will E.?

AGENT FORGETMENOT

TOP SECRET

Forgetmenot Family Birthdays

F = forwards   B = backwards

24th November   29th September

2nd February	3rd May	24th November	29th September
F 1 week	F 6 weeks	F 16 days	F 70 days
B 1 day	B 1 week	B 24 hours	B 1 week
F 6 weeks	F 21 days	F 23 days	B 23 days
B 24 hours	B 24 hours	B 24 hours	B 48 hours
F 14 days	F 28 days	F 25 days	F 28 days
B 48 hours	B 48 hours	F 48 hours	B 96 hours
F 9 days	F 2 weeks and 4 days	B 11 days	F 18 days
F 15 days	B 3 days	F 15 days	B 10 days
B 1 day	B 24 hours	F 48 hours	F 24 hours
Birthday 1	Birthday 2	Birthday 3	Birthday 4

Safe codes

1

Find x. It will always be different.

$x - 10 = 20$

$35 + x = 40$

$x - 40 = 15$

$49 + x = 200$

Add all the values of x.

Double.

2

$x - 66 = 84$

$57 + x = 169$

$x - 80 = 63$

$175 + x = 200$

Add all the values of x.

Double.

3

$x - 205 = 184$

$119 + x = 234$

$x - 80 = 158$

$x + 163 = 240$

Add all the values of x.

Double.

Take away 1000.

20	30	64	16
9	15	200	7

Add the odd numbers together.

Add the multiples of 10.

Add the multiples of 3.

5

20	140	28	18
27	35	36	

Add odd numbers toge[ther]

Add multiples of 10.

Add multiples of 3.

Add multiples o[f]

93	140	28	4
130	24	36	

Add odd numbers togethe[r]

Add multiples of 10.

Add multiples of 3.

Add multiples of 4

Don't Forget:
rs Forgetmenot → middle
f summer
Daughter → closest to
Christmas
Son → end of winter,
beginning of spring
Me → closest to Easter

AGENT FORGETMENOT

3 x 5p

20 x 20p

5 x £5

5 x £1

2 x £10

6

TOP SECRET

These clothes are not actual size. They are for research purposes only. The actual T-shirts shrank to $\frac{1}{2}$ their original size! The trousers shrank to $\frac{1}{4}$ their original size!
Thanks,
M

SPYWEAR

T-shirt		
Size	Length	Chest
Small	52 cm	84 cm
Medium	62 cm	94 cm
Large	72 cm	104 cm

SPYWEAR

Trousers		
Size	Length	Waist
Small	88 cm	74 cm
Medium	98 cm	84 cm
Large	108 cm	94 cm

SNOW WHITE

Gets your clothes sparkling

Washing instructions:
For best results put tablet in
the machine. Use two tablets.
Water temperature must be
hotter than 30°C.
Wash for 90 minutes. If these
instructions are not followed
shrinking may occur.

MRS BUBBLE

SNOW FLAKES

For clothes whiter than white

Washing instructions:
For best results put tablet in
the machine. Use two tablets.
Water temperature must be no
hotter than 30°C.
Wash for no more than 45 minutes.
If these instructions are not
followed shrinking may occur.

Snowflake Enterprises issues warning after disaster hits!

Snow Flakes washing powder claims to
make clothes whiter than white. The
powder now turns white clothes different
colours. Insiders say the powder
ingredients for Snow Flakes have been
mistakenly mixed up. One ingredient in
the secret formula is paint! They mix tiny
amounts of the paints with tap water and
add small amount to each tablet.   They
also add sand and flour! Sources say
workers may have used 4 times as much
of everything as they should have done.
S.E. recommends the powder be used with
coloured clothes only until the problem is
sorted out. Insider sources suggest MI3
will be working on this problem.

Mum M,
- You will need to order school lunches for M junior.
- Make sure she has a different main course every day.
- Each meal should include a meat, a vegetable and a fruit.

Love
Your daughter

Menu du week

roast lamb 80p

chicken salad 75p

lasagne 70p

tabbouleh salad 70p

cheese & tomato pizza 80p

haddock 75p

turkey sausages 30p each

jacket potato with tuna & mayo 50p

chicken pie 70p

vegetable noodles 65p

sweetcorn 20p

cheese & mushroom puff slice 45p

carrots 15p

cheese & spring onion roll 6

mixed vegetables 20p

chicken baguette 60p

salad 25p

fruit yoghurt 21p

roast potatoes 24p

fresh fruit 40p

chunky chips 40p

melon slices with cherri

bread & butter 1

roll & butter 20

Can you find out where the meals are and return them to M Junior's school?

M JUNIOR

What we want for lunch

● = 2 agents

meat (no chicken, not roasted, not in a salad)

lots of vegetables

potatoes (not roasted, no chips)

Italian food (no pasta)

cheese (not with mushrooms)

chicken (not with bread or lettuce)

something creamy with fruit in it

something with vegetables in it

a roasted vegetable

No. of items	Total
4	80p
3	£1·20
2	£1·60
10	£2·50
5	£3·50
3	£2·10
4	£1·60
3	£1·50
5	£1·00

From: Sir Haz Beans
To: M
Subject: Can you find them?

Greetings MI3,

I have hidden clues with the tins of beans.
Which tin? You'll need to work it out.

Clue 1: Bean Enterprises is at the edge of a forest.
Which one? How many ways can you share
36 tins of beans? Find the tin with that number.

Clue 2: 30 tins in groups of 5. How many
groups? Find the tin with that number.

Happy hunting!
Sir Haz Beans

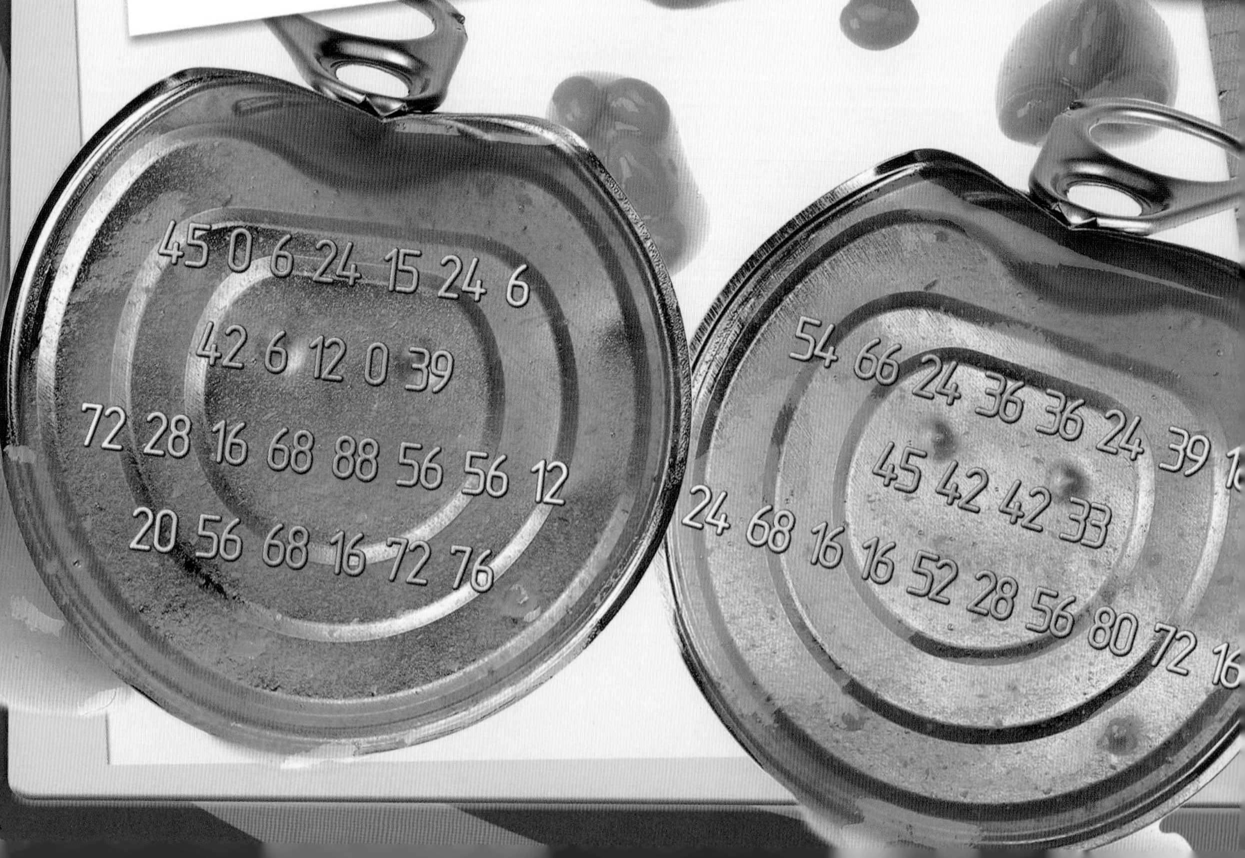

A =
A =

45 0 6 24 15 24 6
42 6 12 0 39
72 28 16 68 88 56 56 12
20 56 68 16 72 76

54 66 24 36 36 24 39 1
45 42 42 33
24 68 16 16 52 28 56 80 72 16

...ear the warehouse there are lots of plants.

B = 3
B = 4

C = 6
C = 8

D = 9...
D = 12...

FREDDY BEANS

SAFE KEYPAD
practice model only

9

WAREHOUSE INFORMATION

- total number of crates = 120
- $\frac{1}{2}$ belong to Sir Haz Beans – those are blue
- $\frac{1}{4}$ that are left contain the meat
- $\frac{1}{3}$ contain the fruit and yoghurt
- $\frac{1}{5}$ contain all the vegetables
- $\frac{1}{10}$ contain the fish

* Must be shipped separately.

Crate transport information

truck 1	truck 3
• 2 rows of 2	• 32 ÷ 4, then take away 4 on bottom row
• 5 high each	• $\frac{1}{4}$ of 16 divided by 2 on top row

truck 2	truck 4
• $\frac{3}{4}$ of 12 on bottom row	• $\frac{1}{4}$ of 20 add 1 on bottom row
• $\frac{2}{3}$ of 9 on top row	• double 8 take away 10 on top row

1
a Put these amounts in order from smallest to largest.

£3·45 69p £3·54 £23·05 £0·68 £32·99

b What is the difference between the smallest and largest amounts?

2
a Will E. got to the bus stop at this time. The bus came 15 minutes later. What time did the bus arrive? Write the time in 2 ways.

His sister, Sheila, arrived 6 minutes earlier and her bus came 10 minutes later than Will E.'s. How long did she spend at the bus stop?

3 M spent £3·75 on a pack of cards. What was her change from £5?

4 Will E. saved £50 of his birthday money. He went to the toy shop and bought a kite for £24·99 and a bag for £6·20. How much money did he have left?

5 Agent Forgetmenot bought his daughter, Sheila, a puzzle for £19·99 and a mouth organ for £7·49. How much did he spend?

6
a Find all the possible ways you can divide these beans with no remainders.

b Write a sharing and a grouping problem for 2 of the ways.

42

Are you ready to move to the next level? Answer these questions to find out. Show your methods in your exercise book.

7 Fill in the missing numbers.

a ☐ + £36 = £45

b ☐ – £15 = £16

c ☐ – £2·50 = £1·75

d £14 + ☐ = £29

e £21 – ☐ = £5

f £10·65 – ☐ = £6·49

8 a Estimate the length and width of the party items.

b Measure to the nearest millimetre.

9 Mrs Bubble mixed this amount of soap with this amount of hot water. How much liquid did she have in total?

10 ➡ Mrs Bubble put a bag of laundry weighing ½ kilo on her scale, and then added a second bag. How much did the second bag weigh?

43

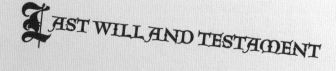

LAST WILL AND TESTAMENT

I, Uncle Mathsamillion, leave my castle to my niece Penny and nephew Les along with all my possessions. I have left you something you will <u>treasure</u> but you will need to <u>shape up</u> first. You will be <u>puzzled</u> at first but once you are <u>clued in</u> all will be clear.

Lots of love,

Uncle Mathsamillion

P.S. Good luck <u>piecing it together</u>. This should help you:

Symmetry is no problem for me.
All my sides are equal, you see—
less than eight but more than three.

I never have an angle wrong,
as my sides are equally long.

What am I?

front gates ➡️

N1 E7 N1 rectangle

Can you find the hidden treasure?

AGENT I.C. SAND

N $\frac{1}{2}$ of 12, divide by 2
quadrilateral, irregular

W = Divide 24 by 6 then add 3
S = Divide 18 by 6 then take away 2
More than 4 sides but no right angles

N = Divide 15 by 3 then take away 4
E = Multiply 4 and 5, what do you need to add to get 23?
just 1 line of symmetry
less than 5 sides

9

The case of the hidden treasure

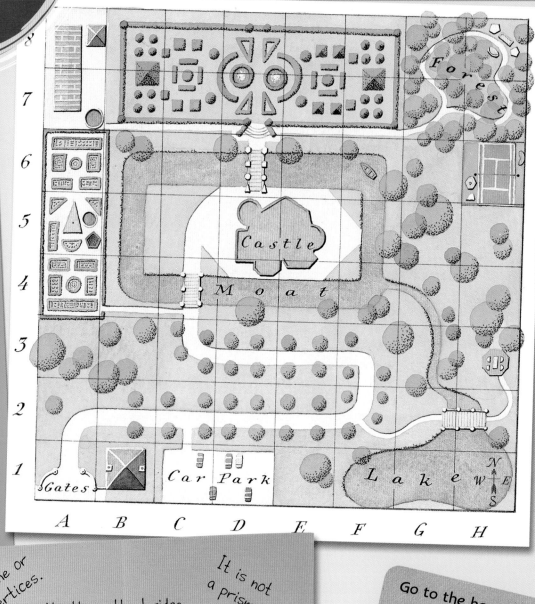

It has one or more vertices.

It is not a prism.

North on the bridge
and down the stairs.
What shapes do you see up in the air?
Time to start digging,
can you guess where?
You must solve these clues,
it's only fair!

It has straight edges.

It is in the west side of the garden.

Go to the hexagon where you find 2 right angles and 1 door.
Walk through to the quadrilateral then choose the one with less than 3 sides.
Start your search.

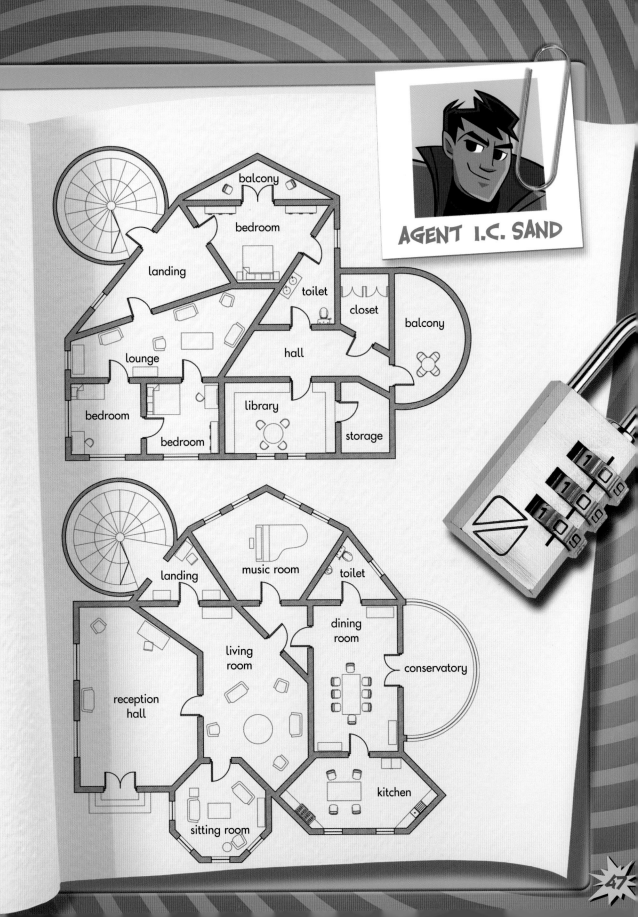

balcony

bedroom

landing

toilet

closet

balcony

lounge

hall

bedroom

library

bedroom

storage

AGENT I.C. SAND

landing

music room

toilet

living room

dining room

conservatory

reception hall

kitchen

sitting room

47

Crockery
(5 of each)

large plate	£3.5
small plate	£2.8
mug	£1.50
cup	£1.00
saucer	50p
bowl	£3.60
serving plate	£4.20

Can you raise the money to buy Jane Blond a super jeep?

JANE BLOND

Electricals
(4 of each)

kettles	£5.00
irons	£4.20
grills	£8.00
plugs	40p
food mixers	£10.80
hair dryers	£3.60
power drills	£12.00

Toys
(6 of each)

teddy bear	£2.50
cuddly toy	£3.80
doll	£3.20
car	80p
farm animal	60p
jigsaw puzzle	£1.50
book	£2.20

Linens
(3 of each)

sheet	£1.00
pillow case	80p
quilt cover	£3.80
blanket	£4.10
curtain	£5.50
tablecloth	£2.80
cushion	£6.00

Clothes (4 of each)

dress	skirt	trousers	shorts	jacket	sweatshirt	T-shirts
£6.40	£4.80	£8.00	£2.50	£10.00	£5.00	£3.50

large £2.00

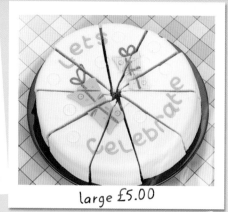
large £5.00

small £1.00

medium £2.50

small 90p

large £3.00

10 for £1.00

large £1.50

small £1.00

M13

Sorry, I seem to have misplaced the completed work timetable. This is all I can remember. I hope it helps so I don't have to start all over again.

Regards,
Agent forgetmenot

0 for £2.00

medium £1.00

small £2.00

JANE BLOND

medium £3.50

medium £3.50

dress £3.20
sheet 50p
kettle £1.25
cup 50p
teddy bear 50p
lower our prices!!!
J.

**** HQ ****
car boot sale
Final Sales

| all cake types and pizzas | 20 x each item |
| biscuits, tea, coffee, pop | 100 x each item |

AUTH CODE
PLEASE
THANK

tea 30p per cup

coffee 40p per mug

soft drink 50p per bottle

Work Timetable
r boot sale day (starts at 10:00 a.m.)

gent	On duty	Shift length
ain	follows Agent Drop	$\frac{2}{3}$ hour
ane Blond	starts first	$\frac{3}{4}$ hour
Quad	before Agent Drop	$\frac{1}{2}$ hour
C. Weed	follows Jane	$\frac{4}{5}$ hour
A. Weed	last	$\frac{9}{10}$ hour
Drop	?	$\frac{1}{4}$ hour

51

1 a Combine these shapes to make as many new shapes as you can.

 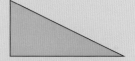

b Name each new shape.

2 Name the shapes and use at least 4 of these words to describe them.

faces
edges
vertices
square
rectangular
triangular

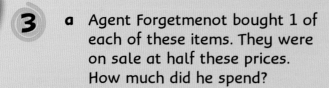

3 a Agent Forgetmenot bought 1 of each of these items. They were on sale at half these prices. How much did he spend?

➡ How much would he have paid if he got another $\frac{1}{4}$ off?

USortIT store

***   ***

egg timer	£4.00
folders	£3.20
paper sorter	£9.00
sticky notes	60p
alarm clock	£1.80
desk tidy	£2.60
organizer	£14.00

PLEASE RETAIN RECEIPT
THANK YOU.

Are you ready to move to the next level? Answer these questions to find out. Show your methods in your exercise book.

4 What fraction of each rectangle is shaded?

a    d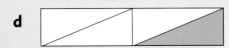

b 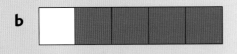   e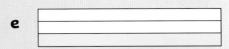

c 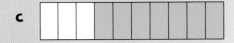   f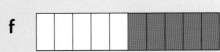

5 a Which of these fractions can you not make with the eggs?

$\dfrac{3}{4}$ $\dfrac{2}{5}$ $\dfrac{1}{2}$ $\dfrac{2}{3}$

➡ What other fractions can you make?

➡ Draw pictures to support your answer.

6 a Solve these.

a 46 + 14   d 56 × 4

b 36 + 29   e 46 ÷ 5

c 102 – 89   f 62 ÷ 10

b Explain your choice of strategy for each one.

46 + 14 =
(40 + 10) + (6 + 4) =
50 + 10 = 60

I added the tens digits first and the units after to make 50 + 10.

What I want for my Super Jee[p]

Desert Hiking Boots
£ 25.00

Battery fan
£ 12.99

Extra-strong windscreen wipers
£ 30.00

Hat & dr[...]
£ 19.9[...]

Furry Dice!

Night-vision binoculars
£ 24.50

Super tyre Pump
£ 13.00

Car Decals £ 7.50

£ 10.50

Listening device
£ 12.99

Flares
£ 15.99

Compass
£ 12.00

Lipstick-shaped digital camera
£ 45.00

Desert camouflage jeep cover
£ 45.00

Desert camouflage driving suit
£ 39.99

SUNSCREEN W/SPARKLES (SPF 40)
£ 2.50

Extra Petro[l] Tan[k]
£ 28.0[...]

Can you get to the bottom of the desert sabotage?

JANE BLOND

AGENT I.C. SAND

Water can
25l
£17

y sunglasses
£12.45

Window sign
£4.25

SPY
ON BOARD

5.00

Covers

MI DEBIT SPYCARD

2468 9753 1357 1591

EXPIRY 10/15

J. BLOND

Mi MATHS INVESTIGATOR

MI3,
Jane's limit
is £200.
M

- HQ to south coast — approximately 150 km
- The Super Jeep has three spare wheels
- We buy our petrol from Eco Petrol Sevices at 20 p per l
- The Super Jeep uses 20 l of petrol every 100 km when it swims
- Jane will drive the Super Jeep to the desert
- The distance across the Mediterranean Sea is 200 km
- The distance across Europe is approximately 1200 km
- The Super Jeep uses 1 l of petrol for every 10 km when it flies

- The distance across The English Channel is 100 km
- Jane will swim the Super Jeep across all water
- Eco Petrol Services is very close to HQ
- From the sea to the desert is approximately 750 km
- Jane is wearing jeans and a T-shirt
- The Super Jeep flies at 200 km per hour
- The Super Jeep swims at 150 km per hour
- The Super Jeep drives at 75 km per hour (or speed limit)
- Jane will fly the Super Jeep across Europe
- The Super Jeep uses 10 l of petrol for every 100 km when it drives

55

From: Jane Blond
To: M
Subject: clues for coordinate and code key A=1   B=2   C=3 …

Hi M,

Here are the clues to find out each month and the code key I received.
Good luck to MI3! I am counting on them.

Jane

PS You'll need to use a 2006 calendar.

1
1. even number of days
2. only 1 Wednesday is a multiple of 3
3. only 1 weekend day is a multiple of 10

2
1. odd number of days
2. equal number of odd Fridays as even
3. 1 Thursday is a multiple of 3, the other 4
4. 1 weekend day is a multiple of 3 and 10

3
1. more than 8 weekend days
2. 2 Mondays are multiples of 3
3. more odd Sundays than even
4. towards the end of the year

4
1. 4 Wednesdays
2. only 1 Tuesday is a multiple of 3
3. even number of days
4. last day of month falls on the day of the week before the day of the week of the first day of the month

5
1. 8 weekend days
2. 5 Wednesdays
3. some Wednesdays are multiples of 2, 3, 4, 5, and/or 10
4. 1 Friday is a multiple of 3 and 6

Agent Blond
Congratulations on making it this far, Agent Blond. Completing this task will bring you several steps closer to your friend, I.C.

Find your way through the palace and see how many carpets you can collec You need to get as many as possibl but you may only visit each room o

in	2	4	5	6
	8	7	10	9
	8	10	6	
	4	6	8	

Happy hunting!
Sue Veneer

Each face represents 4 people
What people chose
        T-shirts
30   tea glasses
48   soft toy camels
54   postcards
35   coin purses

JANE BLOND

AGENT I.C. SAND

soft toy camels		☺☺☺☺☺☺☺☺☺☺☺ ☺☺☺☺☺☺☺☺☺
tea glasses		
coin purses		☺☺☺☺☺☺☺☺☺☺☺ ☺☺☺
postcards		☺☺☺☺☺☺☺☺☺
T-shirts		☺☺☺☺☺☺☺☺☺☺☺☺☺ ☺☺☺☺☺☺☺☺☺☺☺☺

Supply Store prices

Item	BestBuy	BettaBuy	BeatIt	SoLow
coin purses	2 for £3	£1.99 each	3 for £4.50	£1.80 each
T-shirts	2 for £5	£2.49 each	£2.99 each	3 for £7.50
postcards	2 for 36p	5 for £1.20	4 for £1.00	18p each
soft toy camels	£1.99 each	2 for £3.00	5 for £10.00	4 for £8
tea glasses	2 for 90p	39p each	5 for £3.50	3 for £3.00

TOP SECRET

M and MI3,

Thanks for the help with transporting the you-know-whats. Best we communicate in code from now on since we don't want 'them' to find out too much.

Cheers,

Noah Sark

PS I hope you get the picture when you look at the film.

FYI for later: The digit total for each animal code matches a shape.

1
doub...
64 – ?
19 + 9
$\frac{1}{2}$ of 28
23 + 19
$\frac{1}{4}$ of 72
15 + 13
$\frac{1}{2}$ of 76

2
53 – 29
$\frac{3}{4}$ of 32
16 ÷ 8
17 + 9
$\frac{2}{3}$ of 3

3
double 7 + 8
double 15
124 – 122
15 + 9
14 ÷ 7
24 ÷ 6
70 ÷ 7
$\frac{1}{5}$ of 10
100 – 64

4
100 – 62
19 + 9
100 ÷ 50
50 – 28
43 – 33

5
$\frac{1}{2}$ of 28
9 x 2
25 + 11
50 – 48
24 ÷ 2
$\frac{1}{3}$ of 36
$\frac{1}{5}$ of 50

A = 2
B = 4
C = 6
D = 8

M
HQ
...ar...
UK...

World Cup Winners

Can you get the animals safely to their destination?

NOAH SARK

FOOD
FOR *1*
FEEDING

●		▲	
krill	500g	acacia	2kg
squid	250g	hay	1kg
fish	1kg	carrots	500g

▭		⬠		⬡	
slugs	250g	eucalyptus	1.5kg	grass	750g
birds	400g	mistletoe	450g	hay	1kg
mice	300g	tree bark	100g	hedges	500g

4 feedings each day

TOP SECRET

Size table

'Shapes'	length	height	width
▭	1.4 m	10 cm	12 cm
▲	1.5 m	5.4 m	75 cm
⬠	75 cm	50 cm	40 cm
⬡	1.2 m	2 m	75 cm
●	50 cm	1 m	40 cm

Sleeping quarters need to be:
- twice as long as they are
- $\frac{1}{2}$ as high again
- 4 times as wide

Water

☐ millilitres every hour

◁ millilitres every hour

▱ millilitres every hour

⬡ millilitres every hour

○ millilitres every hour

Travel Schedule

NOAH SARK

6:00 a.m.	Leave Coventry for London 2 h 50 min
	London to Dover 2 h 10 min
	Dover to Calais 1 h 45 min
	Calais to Beauvais 1 h 50 min
	Beauvais to Paris 35 min
	Paris to Orleans 55 min
	Orleans to Limoges 2 h 25 min
	Limoges to Toulouse 3 h 35 min
Arrive?	Toulouse to Narbonne 1 h 50 min

TOP SECRET

The neighbours' favourite fruit

strawberries	18
blackberries	17
mangoes	28
plums	32
papayas	21
passion fruits	23
gooseberries	9
blueberries	12

Mr Plum's friends' favourite fruits

Number of friends

30, 28, 26, 24, 22, 20, 18, 16, 14, 12, 10, 8, 6, 4, 2, 0

kiwis, pears, apples, peaches, grapes, pineapples, cherries, grapefruits

Type of Fruit

Can you help Mr Plum set up his fruit shop?

What people think about oranges and lemons

	like oranges	don't like oranges
like lemons	Sue Karen Romone Lok Beyant Fen Ali	Cori Kimiko Arwa Laura
don't like lemons	Kirby John Gillian Ula Zia Patrick	Brian Hamish

MR PLUM

People who like bananas and blackcurrants

like blackcurrants   like bananas

The case of Mr Plum's plans

STRAWBERRIES
£1.10 a basket

PLUMS

4 for 76p

MANGOES

63p each

PAPAYAS

2 for 80p

Fruit order
for Mrs Singh

4 mangoes

2 pears

6 kiwis

5 baskets of
strawberries

$\frac{1}{2}$ kilo cherries

2 plums

250 g grapes

4 pineapples

KIWI FRUITS
3 for £1.05

MR PLUM

GRAPES
£1.26 for 500g

CHERRIES
£4.45 for kg

PASSION FRUITS
54p each

PINEAPPLES
£1.45 each

PEARS
3 for 36p

65

Agent security clearance

TOP SECRET

1 Copy and complete this table.

Number →	Round to →	Round to
3 ☐ 6	390	☐ ☐ ☐
☐ 34	☐ 30	400
1 ☐ 9	2 ☐ ☐	☐ ☐ ☐
53 ☐	540	☐ ☐ ☐

386 → 390 → 400

£22·75 £9·48 £8·50 £12·50

£7·25 £4·56 £18·25 £17·50

2
a I.C. Sand bought Jane a travel mug and a vase. How much did he spend?

b He paid with £20 pound note. How much change did he get?

c IC Sand also bought 2 things for himself which cost a total of around £40. What did he buy?

3 How much would they have to pay in total?

a 4 children
b 3 families
c 2 adults
d 5 seniors

Admission prices
child 40p
family £1·70
adult 95p
senior 20p

Are you ready to move to the next level? Answer these questions to find out. Show your methods in your exercise book.

Visitors to Noah Sark's Sanctuary

Use a ruler or your finger to guide you.

4
a How many visitors did he have altogether?

b What is the difference between the number of weekday visitors and weekend vistors?

c Order the days of the week from most to least popular.

favourite animal

animal	votes
hedgehog	IIII
fox	III
rabbit	IIIIIII
donkey	IIIII
owl	II

5
a How many visitors liked rabbits more than donkeys?

b How many visitors voted?

➲ Use the information from this tally chart to make a pictogram.

6
a Copy and complete the table.

1·4 m	1 m 40 cm	140 cm
	2 m 35 cm	
5·23 m		
		325 cm

➲ Measure the length of three large objects in your classroom. Make a table like this one to show your findings.

The case of the secret present

sapphire

opal

Prices for gemstones

Precious stones	Small	Medium	Large
Sapphires	£152	£211	£305
Opals	£78	£120	£147
Diamonds	£75	£106	£157
Emeralds	£92	£124	£171
Rubies	£65	£99	£115
Amethysts	£80	£130	£175

diamond

emerald

14 The case of the secret present

MI3,

I went with the least expensive jeweller
you suggested. I decided on 1 medium
stone of each type, cut in 2. Here are
the shapes I chose. What pattern do you
suggest for the bracelet?
Jane

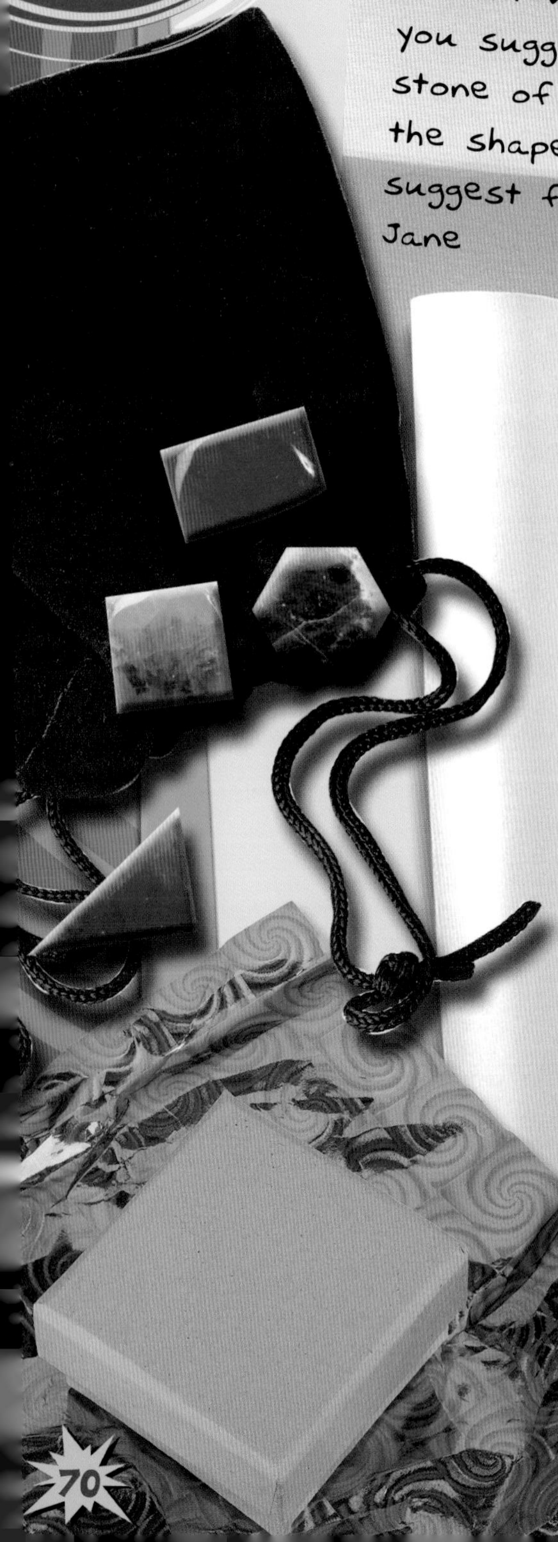

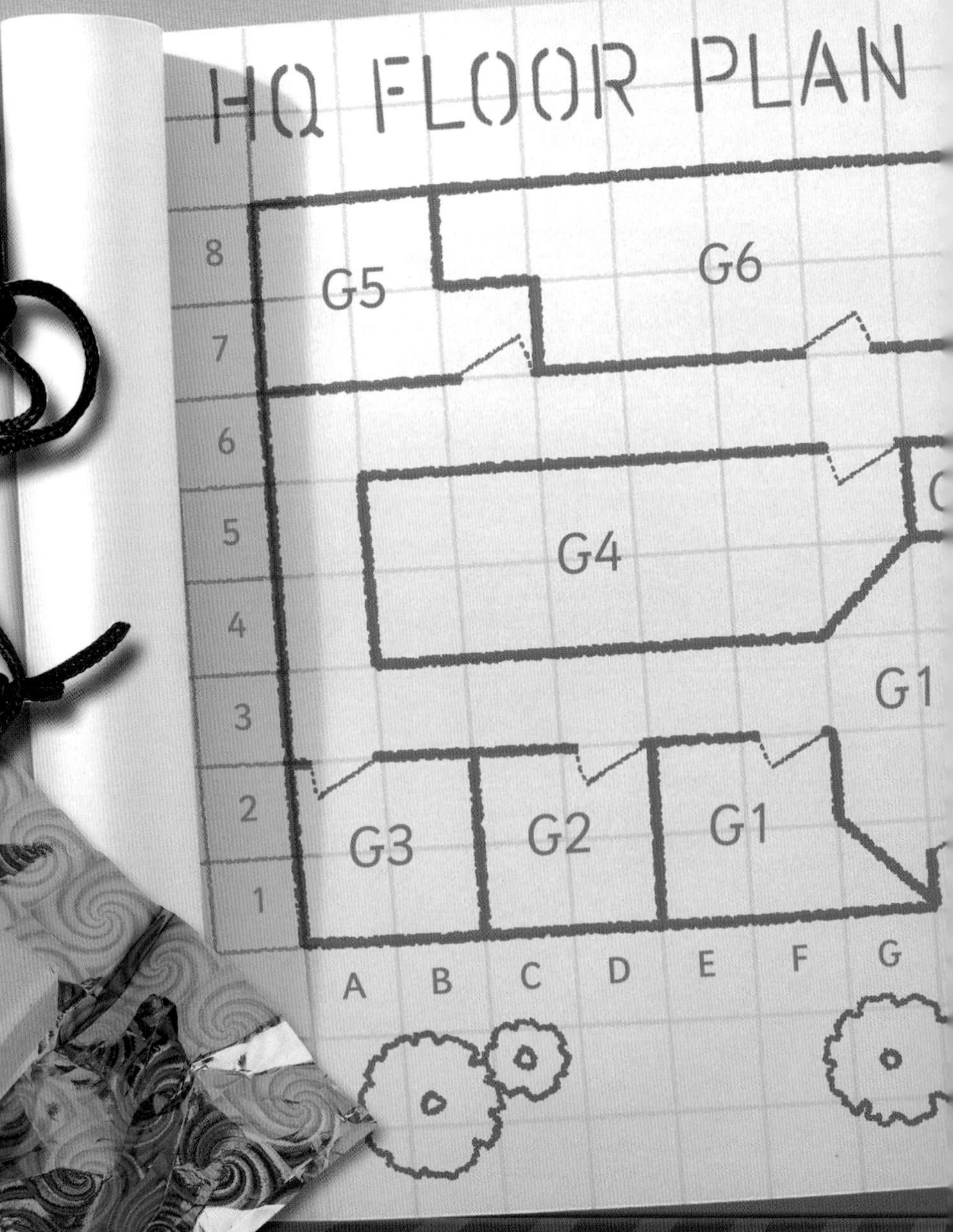

HQ FLOOR PLAN
G5
G6
G4
G1
G3
G2
G1
8
7
6
5
4
3
2
1
A
B
C
D
E
F
G

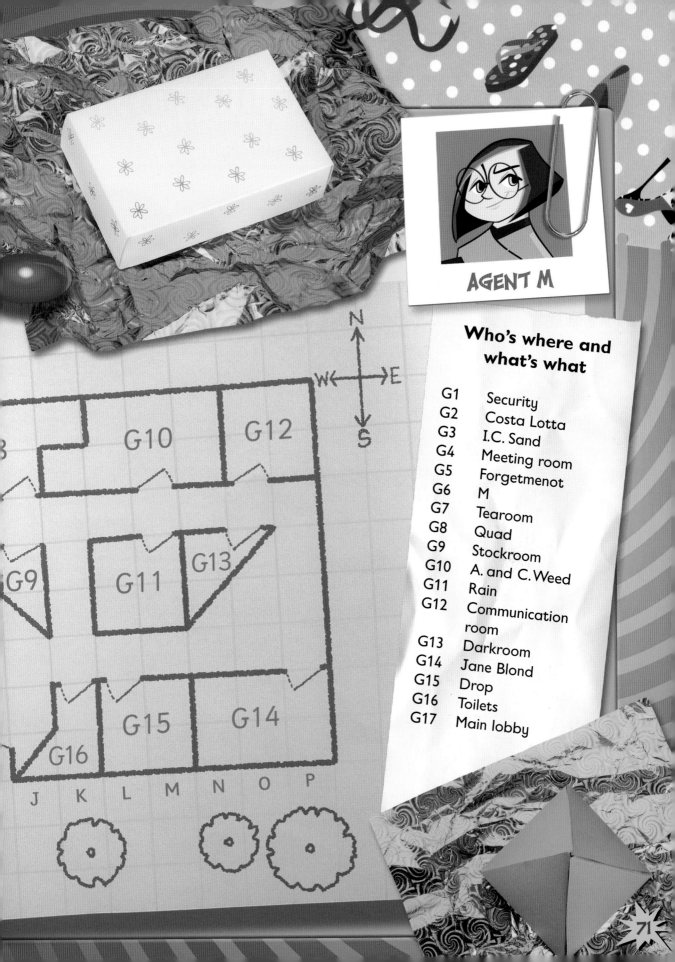

N
W ← → E
S

AGENT M

G10   G12

G9   G11   G13

G15   G14

G16

J K L M N O P

Who's where and what's what

G1	Security
G2	Costa Lotta
G3	I.C. Sand
G4	Meeting room
G5	Forgetmenot
G6	M
G7	Tearoom
G8	Quad
G9	Stockroom
G10	A. and C. Weed
G11	Rain
G12	Communication room
G13	Darkroom
G14	Jane Blond
G15	Drop
G16	Toilets
G17	Main lobby

FORM LETTER

Dear _____ :

We are pleased to offer you a position here as an Agent with MI. You will be paid £3 an hour. Here are the general working hours that all agents must follow.

You will:

- work 35–40 hours a week
- have at least 1 day off a week
- work no more than 10 hours a day
- work no less than 4 hours a day

These rules do not apply to special occasions or secret missions. Welcome to our team!

Happy investigating,

M

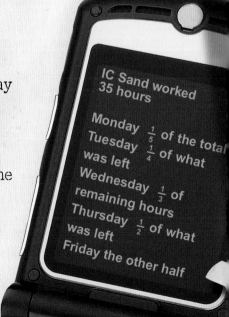

IC Sand worked 35 hours

Monday $\frac{1}{5}$ of the total
Tuesday $\frac{1}{4}$ of what was left
Wednesday $\frac{1}{3}$ of remaining hours
Thursday $\frac{1}{2}$ of what was left
Friday the other half

Agents Rain and Drop

Hours worked: 40 each
- $\frac{1}{2}$ of the hours at the weekend ($\frac{3}{10}$ on Sunday, rest on Saturday with overtime)
- $\frac{1}{2}$ of the hours during week ($\frac{1}{5}$ Tuesday, $\frac{2}{5}$ Wednesday, rest on Thursday)

MONEY EARNED

Agent	A. Weed	C. Weed
Monday	£12	£21
Tuesday	£30	£18
Wednesday	£18	£30
Thursday	£21	£18
Friday	£27	£0
Saturday	£0	£24
Sunday	£0	£0

Name: _____ Date: _____

Time/Day	Monday	Tuesday	Wednesday	Thursday	Friday	Saturday	Sunday
8:00 – 9:00	start?						
9:00 – 10:00							
10:00 –11:00							
11:00 –12:00							
12:00 –1:00	lunch?						
1:00 – 2:00							
2:00 – 3:00							
3:00 – 4:00							
4:00 – 5:00							
5:00 – 6:00	finish?						
6:00 – 7:00							
7:00 – – 8:00							
8:00 – 9:00							
9:00 – 10:00							
10:00 – 11:00							
11:00 – 12:00							

Hi MI3,

I worked 40 hours.

Monday: $\frac{1}{10}$ of my hours

Tuesday: $\frac{1}{4}$ of remaining hours

Wednesday: $\frac{1}{3}$ of remaining hours

Thursday: $\frac{1}{2}$ of that

Friday: $\frac{2}{3}$ of what was left

Saturday: all the rest

Cheers!

Mrs Bubble

COSTA LOTTA

Agent	Started	Lunch Break	Coffee Break
C. Weed	9:00 a.m.	1 hour	no
Quad	7:30 a.m.	no	10 minutes x 6
A. Weed	same time as Rain	50 minutes	no

Agents who didn't eat lunch

Mrs Bubble

I.C. Sand

Forgetmenot

Fry-up

Costa Lotta

Rain

Drop

Hi MI3,

More info about Agents' weeks:
- I started half an hour before midday and took 3 half-hour breaks.
- Mrs Bubble started 15 minutes after I.C. Sand.
- I.C. Sand started 10 minutes before C. Weed.
- Forgetmenot started work 15 minutes after Rain. He forgot to take a break, of course!
- Fry-up started 20 minutes before Quad. He took a 40-minute break after serving lunch.
- Rain started work 2 hours before I.C. Sand and took three 15-minute breaks.
- Drop started at the same time as Rain and took two 45-minute breaks every day.

Thanks again,
Costa

Agent security clearance

1 **a** Use these 5 triangles to make as many different shapes as you can.

b Draw and name each new shape.

c Find how many lines of symmetry each new shape has.

2 Match each statement to one of these 3D shapes.

cuboid	a prism, 2 circular faces
cone	5 vertices
pyramid	1 vertex, a rounded face
cylinder	no faces, no vertex
cube	12 edges, faces all the same
sphere	a prism, with 6 faces in two sizes

3 Agent Quad is designing a decorative belt pattern. Make 6 patterns using these shapes.

4 Write directions from the car park to the jeweller's shop for Jane Blond to follow.

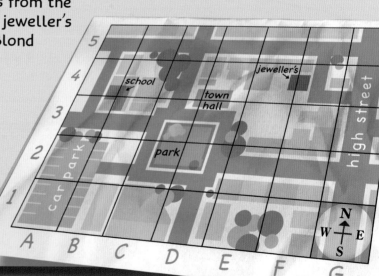

Are you ready to move to the next level? Answer these questions to find out. Show your methods in your exercise book.

5   **a**   Find $\frac{1}{2}$ of these numbers.

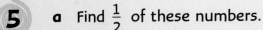

     b   Find $\frac{1}{4}$.

     ➲ Which numbers can be evenly divided into thirds?

6   Order these fractions on a number line from smallest to largest.

$$\frac{1}{2} \qquad \frac{9}{10} \qquad \frac{1}{8} \qquad \frac{3}{4} \qquad \frac{1}{4} \qquad \frac{1}{3}$$

7   How many parts need to be shaded to show each fraction?

     a $\frac{2}{2}$ **c** $\frac{4}{5}$

     b $\frac{1}{2}$ **d** $\frac{2}{3}$

8   This is when Agents Rain, Drop and Quad arrived at the airport.

     a   Agent Rain arrived 2 and $\frac{3}{4}$ hours before her flight. When was her flight?

     b   Agent Quad arrived 1 $\frac{1}{2}$ hours before his flight and it was delayed by 40 minutes. When did it take off?

     ➲ Agent Drop's flight was delayed only $\frac{1}{4}$ of that time. How long was her flight delayed?

9   Answer these. Show at least 2 different strategies.

     a   156 + 54   **c**   24 × 4

     b   148 – 98   **d**   56 ÷ 10

Useful codewords

a.m. – short for *ante meridiem* meaning 'before noon', used to show times between 12 midnight and 12 noon

analogue clock – a clock that has hands to show the passing of time

angle – an amount of turn; flat shapes have angles at the corners

anti-clockwise – turns in the direction opposite to the hands on a clock

approximate answer – a rough answer or estimate near to the exact answer

array – a regular arrangement of objects in rows and columns

axis (axes) – graphs have two axes, one horizontal and one vertical

bar chart – a graph that uses bars or columns to show information

capacity – the amount a container holds, measured in l and ml

Carroll diagram – used for sorting things into groups, e.g. red and not red, cubes and not cubes

century – a set of one hundred, e.g. 100 years

clockwise – turns in the same direction as hands on a clock

column – a vertical line of objects or numbers one above the other

compass points – a compass is used to find directions; north (N), south (S), east (E) and west (W) are the four main points on a compass

data – information about something in words, numbers or pictures

diagonal – a straight line that joins two corners of a shape

digit – each figure in a number is called a digit, e.g. 26 is called a 2-digit number

Useful codewords

digital clock – a clock that has only numbers to show the time

edge – the edge is where two faces of a solid shape meet, e.g. a cube has 12 straight edges

equivalent fractions – fractions with the same value, e.g. $\frac{2}{4} = \frac{1}{2}$

estimate – using information you have to guess an answer without measuring or doing a difficult calculation

even number – any whole number that can be divided exactly by 2, e.g. 2, 4, 6, 8, 10 ...

face – a side of a solid shape, e.g. a cube has 6 square faces

frequency – how often something happens

horizontal – a level or flat line parallel to the horizon or ground, a line parallel to the bottom edge when represented on paper

inverse – the opposite; addition and subtraction are inverse operations

line symmetry – a shape has line symmetry if it can be folded so one half covers the other exactly

mass – the amount of matter in an object, measured in g or kg (sometimes people use weight to mean mass)

mid-point – halfway between two points

multiple – a number that is exactly divisible by another, e.g. numbers in the times table 5, 10, 15, 20, 25, 30 are all multiples of 5

negative numbers – numbers less than zero

net – a 2-D shape that can be folded up to make a 3-D shape

odd number – any whole number that cannot be divided exactly by 2, e.g. 1, 3, 5, 7, 9, 11 ...

Useful codewords

p.m. – short for *post meridiem* meaning 'after noon', used to show times between 12 noon and 12 midnight

partition – to break numbers down into, e.g. units, tens and hundreds

pictogram – a graph that uses pictures to show information

predict – to say what you think will happen

positive numbers – numbers greater than zero

product – the answer when two or more numbers are multiplied together, e.g. the product of 4 and 8 is 32

quadrilateral – a polygon with four sides

reflection – the mirror image of a shape

remainder – the number left over after division, e.g. $7 \div 3 = 2 \text{ r } 1$

right angle – a quarter turn measured as an angle of $90°$

row – a horizontal line of objects or numbers side by side

round up/down – writing a number as an approximate, e.g. 64 rounded to the nearest ten is 60

sequence – a set of numbers written in an order following a rule, e.g. 1, 4, 7, 10 is a sequence adding 3 each time

Venn diagram – used for sorting things into sets

vertical – a line that points straight up at right angles to a horizontal line; a line parallel to the sides when represented on paper

vertex (vertices) – the corner of a shape, where sides or straight edges meet